Johannes Brahms

Clarinet Sonata No.2

Op.120 No.2

A Score for Clarinet and Piano

British Library Cataloguing-in-Publication Data
A catalogue record for this book is available from
the British Library

Sonate Nr. 2

für Klarinette (oder Bratsche) und Pianoforte

Johannes Brahms, Op. 120 Nr. 2
(Veröffentlicht 1895)

12

14

18

21

CPSIA information can be obtained
at www.ICGtesting.com
Printed in the USA
BVOW11s1951280118

505519BV00016B/227/P